To

_____

From

_____

Date

_____

WHO IS GOD?

By Kathleen Ruckman
Illustrated by Greg Hardin and Robert Vann

HARVEST HOUSE PUBLISHERS

EUGENE, OREGON

Scripture quotations are taken from the New King James Version.
Copyright ©1982 by Thomas Nelson, Inc. Used by permission. All rights reserved.

WHO Is GOD?

Text Copyright © 2010 by Kathleen Ruckman
Artwork Copyright © 2010 by Greg Hardin and Robert Vann

Published by Harvest House Publishers
Eugene, Oregon 97402
www.harvesthousepublishers.com

ISBN 978-0-7369-2570-9

Original illustrations by Greg Hardin

Design and production by Mary pat Design, Westport, Connecticut

Printed in China

10 11 12 13 14 15 16 / LP / 10 9 8 7 6 5 4 3 2 1

With gratitude to my parents for the Christian home where I grew up in Pennsylvania...In memory of my mother, Susan, who's in heaven, and to my father, Samuel, who is still teaching his children to "whistle while you work."
—Kathleen Ruckman

Soli Deo Gloria

For my nephews Andrew and Colton, and my niece Charlotte.
—Greg Hardin

Annie and Adam love to visit Grandpa on Sundays, especially during the summer because they get to have sleepovers.

"Grandpa!" squeals Annie as she leaps into his arms. "We're back!"

"Hey, Grandpa, can we camp out in the hayloft tonight?" asks Adam, not wasting one minute.

"If it's okay with your mom and dad, you can sleep in the hayloft," answers Grandpa.

Mom and Dad think it's a great idea and give the children and Grandpa a hug before saying goodbye.

Annie and Adam arrive hungry because they know Grandpa is a good cook, and they always wonder what he'll make for supper when they visit.

Grandpa doesn't keep them in suspense. "Tonight we'll have spaghetti and meatballs, and then cookies with milk for dessert." Annie helps set the table while Grandpa stirs the spaghetti sauce.

Adam moves his head around and around as he twirls and twirls his spaghetti on his fork. And just when Adam is about to eat a fork full of spaghetti, Grandpa says, "Are we forgetting something, Adam?"

"Grandma said to always thank God for the food we eat!" Annie tells Adam. "Grandpa, may I pray?"

Grandpa nods yes.

"Dear God, thank You for our spaghetti, for the cows that gave us the milk, and for the meatballs too. Thank You for Grandpa and for Grandma in heaven. Amen."

After dinner, Grandpa, Annie, and Adam go out for a stroll and head for the barn.

"Grandpa, can Stanley camp out with us in the hayloft?" Annie asks. "He's a good watchdog."

"If we can get him up the steps, he can," Grandpa replies. "But before we get you two and Stanley settled in, I'll make some popcorn and we'll watch the sun go down and the stars come out."

Not long after Grandpa brings out the popcorn, the sun sets in the sky like a big orange ball.

"Hey! That sun looks like my basketball!" shouts Adam as he slam-dunks the ball into the hoop on Grandpa's barn. "Can we go campin' now?"

When they all get to the top, Grandpa sets down the sleeping bags and throws open the shutters to a view of the night sky.

"Look at the stars, Grandpa. They look like diamonds!" Annie exclaims.

There are lots of lightning bugs on Grandpa's Pennsylvania farm in the summer. Adam catches one and puts it in an empty jelly jar with holes punched in the lid.

"The fireflies look like little stars dancing for us," giggles Annie.

"All the stars that you see are in our Milky Way Galaxy," explains Grandpa. "Did you know that our sun is actually a star and that there are gazillions of stars and galaxies beyond the Milky Way that our eyes can't see? The Bible says that God calls every star by name. And He know you *too,* Annie and Adam, by name!"

"Wow! Look at those stars over there. They look like the ladle for our spaghetti sauce!" yells Adam.

"That constellation, or arrangement of stars, is called the *Big Dipper* because it's shaped like a big serving spoon," says Grandpa. "The Bible says the heavens are filled with many wonders, and that the universe is God's handiwork. It's like the fingers of an artist made it all, and that artist is God!"

"Grandpa, who is God?" asks Adam.

Grandpa's forehead *really* wrinkles when he thinks hard. "Now that's a BIG question, because God is so awesome!

"First of all, God is our Creator. He made all that we see around us. The Bible says, 'In the beginning God created the heavens and the earth.' "

"But who made God?" Annie asks.

"No one made God, Annie," Grandpa answers. His blue eyes twinkle like the stars.

"Then did God make Himself?" asks Adam.

"God did not make Himself," explains Grandpa. "God has no beginning and no end. God said, 'Let there be light.' And then there was light. He created everything—heaven, earth, and all living things. The Bible says we see how *awesome* God is by looking at His creation. He is the *only* one who can make something out of nothing."

"Even Cleveland!" exclaims Annie as she hugs the big cat that looks like a little tiger. "Grandpa, where is God? Is He up there...in heaven?"

"Yes, He's up in heaven—but He's here on earth too. In fact, God is *everywhere.* He's the *only* one who can be everywhere all the time."

"You mean God is in the leaves and rocks and stars?" asks Adam.

"Oh no!" says Grandpa. "God *made* the rocks, leaves, stars, and all that we see in nature. But He's *not* the stars, rocks, or leaves. He is able to be everywhere at all times because He alone is God! God knows and understands *everything,* and He always knows what's best. The Bible says God is so wise that no one has to teach Him."

"God is *awesome!*" says Adam as he catches one more firefly.

"No one is as smart as God! Not even Ben in school, who gets all A's!" Annie says, joining in.

"This *awesome* God is your heavenly Father, and He loves it when you talk to Him," Grandpa tells the children. "And did you know that God hears the prayers of all the children all over the world, even if they're said at the same time? Speaking of prayer, it's now time to say our prayers and go to sleep.

"Dear heavenly Father, help Annie and Adam to know how much You love them, deeper than the ocean and higher than the sky. Help them to know You are *with them* every second of every day and night. Thank You that Annie and Adam came to see me again so we can enjoy each other's company and learn more about You on this wonderful evening. Amen."

"I'll leave the kitchen door open in case you need to come in," says Grandpa.

"OR, in case we want more cookies and milk!" says Adam.

"Good night, Grandpa," whispers Annie, curling up inside her sleeping bag with Stanley. "It's fun to spend the night and talk about God."

"See you in the morning," Adam says, yawning.

Crickets chirp and frogs croak, and soon Annie and Adam are fast asleep.

The morning sun rises behind the hills on Grandpa's farm. Annie and Adam are in a deep sleep...until an annoying sound wakes them up.

"Oh no! Not that rooster again!" grumbles Adam as he puts his head under his pillow.

Annie and Adam eventually get up, and head toward the house to wash up for breakfast. They find Grandpa sitting in his favorite chair where he reads his Bible in the mornings.

"Good morning, kids!" says Grandpa. "Since we're all up, do you want to go fishing? The fish like to bite early in the morning."

"YES!" shouts Adam. He gulps down his cereal and runs to the shed to get Grandpa's fishing box.

When they get to Grandpa's river dock, Grandpa helps put worms on their fishing hooks. One by one, they drop their lines in the water.

"We might have to wait awhile," says Grandpa. "But that's the fun of it. People are always doing *something,* and sometimes it's fun to just do *nothing.*"

"Grandpa, can we talk more about God while we wait for the fish to bite?" asks Annie.

"Sure we can. I love to talk about God," he answers as he sits in his lawn chair.

"Grandpa, if God created everything, do you mean God even created WORMS?" asks Adam.

"Yes, even worms," chuckles Grandpa. "You see, everything has a purpose. The Bible says that in every season there is a special purpose and plan—like when we use these worms as bait to catch fish, when I harvest the corn in the fall, and when I let the land rest in the wintertime."

Just then something pulls on Adam's fishing line! "Whoaaaa!" he shouts as he leans backward and turns the reel. "I caught a FISH!" Adam reels in the fish, and as he tries to take it off the hook, the fish wiggles and jumps back into the water!

Annie giggles and shakes her head at Adam just as she spies a ladybug along the dock.

"Grandpa, why did God put dots on a ladybug's back?" she asks.

"Annie, I'm so happy you notice tiny things. It's so easy to miss these small blessings. I'll bet God put those dots there to make the ladybug special just like He did when He put freckles on Adam!" Grandpa says with a tender smile.

"Grandpa, you sure love to talk about God!" says Annie.

"I do because I love Him—and He loves me. The Bible says that if we had a grain of sand for each time God thinks of us, we would have more sand than there is in the entire world!"

"Awesome!" says Adam. "There are *zillions* of grains of sand, and more grains washing up on the shore every day. God must think about us all day long!"

"That's right," says Grandpa. "God loves us SO much. We are never out of His sight, and we are always on His mind."

Grandpa looks up at the sunrise. "The sun rises just as night will come again," he tells the kids. "Things are always changing—seasons change, people change and grow up and grow old, and even your shadow changes moment by moment. But God never changes."

Grandpa puts his arms around the children. "Always remember when things change so fast and life gets so hard, God is the one Person who never ever changes. You can always count on Him. He is like the anchor on the boat. God holds on to you—and His love will never let you go."

"Yes, we'll remember!" Annie says. "Grandpa, may we go gather eggs now? I want to see Clara!"

"Sure, Annie," replies Grandpa. "Let's pack up and put away our gear before we head to the chicken coop. Well, fishing was fun even if we didn't get any fish to take home. Being together is what counts."

The chicken coop is a noisy, crazy place where chickens run and scatter.

"Hey, what came first, the chicken or the egg? I heard someone ask that one time," asks Adam.

"The chicken!" shouts Annie, quite sure of herself. "Because God made all the animals *first*! THEN the chicken laid the egg!"

Grandpa smiles, happy with Annie's answer.

Just then Annie sees a fuzzy baby chick poking its head out from under its mother's wing. "Oh, Grandpa, look!" she says tenderly.

"Annie and Adam, did you know the Bible says we are like little chicks under the wings of God? They're not wings like a mother bird's wings, but God uses this example to let us know we are safe in His care. And that's where He wants us to rest and trust Him—like this baby bird trusts its mother."

"I'm God's little chick." Annie smiles as she strolls out of the chicken coop, gently swinging her basket of eggs.

On the way back to the house, Annie notices the daisies in the field and asks if they could sit down for a while so she can make a daisy chain.

"Sure! It's a good time to rest. You know, Grandma loved daisies too," says Grandpa with a smile so bright it made him look young again.

Adam lays down in the soft grass, looks up at the sky, and asks, "Grandpa, is Jesus God?"

"That's a great question, Adam," answers Grandpa. "The Bible tells us that when we see Jesus, we also see God, and if we know Jesus, we also know God. It's like you and your dad. You two are so much alike. To see and know you is like seeing and knowing your dad. *God the Father* wants us to know Him, and so He sent His only Son from heaven to

live with us on earth as an ordinary man so we can get to know Him better. At Christmas we celebrate God's Son's birthday. You see, it was *God the Son* who was born in a manger in Bethlehem. And His name is..."

"Jesus!" shouts Adam. "You mean God who made the universe came down to earth?"

"Yes," answers Grandpa. "If you study the Bible, you'll learn that the only way to live with God forever in heaven is to live a perfect life without *sinning*. Sinning is doing and thinking bad things. Though Jesus lived as a man, He never sinned. He taught us how to live a perfect life without sin but knew that we could not. So God the Father sent God the Son to die on the cross so that all of our sins may be forgiven."

"Tell us about the cross, Grandpa," asks Annie.

"The Bible says God is love," says Grandpa. "Jesus loves us so much that He willingly died on a cross for each of us. The cross is like a bridge from God's perfect heaven to our imperfect lives. Jesus, through dying on the cross, created the only bridge that we can take to live in God's perfect heaven forever, no matter how many bad things we've thought or done.

"But Jesus didn't stay dead. He conquered death and came back to life three days later! That's what Easter is all about. Jesus tells us that He is now in heaven preparing our eternal home, but He didn't leave us all alone on earth. God sent His Holy Spirit to live inside all who have accepted Jesus as the only bridge to heaven! So now you know there is God the Father, God the Son, and God the Holy Spirit—the Holy Trinity, three persons in one God."

"When I say my prayers, I'm going to tell Jesus thank You," says Annie.

"When we know Jesus is alive and His Spirit lives in our hearts, every day is like Easter," Grandpa replies.

"Look, a Monarch!" Grandpa points out. "Only God could paint such bright colors and designs. This butterfly was once in a dark cocoon, but look at it now!

"Annie and Adam, we are like that butterfly when we welcome God into our hearts and lives. The Creator of heaven and earth wants to create new hearts in us so we can be more like Jesus! God promises to live in our hearts and be our Helper and Friend!"

Annie places the daisy garland in her hair, just like Grandma did long ago, and begins to dance through the flowers.

Grandpa picks up Annie's basket of eggs, and the three of them walk back toward Grandpa's house. Annie hops onto the old farm swing that hangs from an apple tree as Adam throws a large stick at its trunk, trying to knock down some apples—and an apple falls right on his head!

"Ouch!" he shouts as both Grandpa and Annie can hardly hold in their laughter.

Ginger the horse trots toward the fence, and Adam gives her an apple. Stanley barks at Sam, the mailman, who drops a letter into the mailbox.

"Grandpa, you sure know a lot about God," says Annie as they walk into the house for lunch.

"God is so wonderful! I can only describe Him the best I can from what I've learned in the Bible," Grandpa tells the kids as he carefully puts the eggs in used egg cartons.

"Like the letters Sam delivered, God gave us the Bible. The Bible is like a love letter to us from God. When we read the Bible, we learn about God and who He is. The Bible is unlike any other book, and its truths are forever because it comes straight from God."

"Can you tell us some Bible stories when we visit next time?" Annie asks.

"I sure can," Grandpa says with a happy twinkle in his eyes.

Grandpa, Annie, and Adam hear the loud Pennsylvania thunder crackle and rumble in the distance as they eat their lunch.

"I won't be afraid when it thunders because God is with me," Annie tells Grandpa.

"Me too," says Adam.

All too soon, Mom and Dad arrive to take Annie and Adam home.

Adam gives Grandpa a quick hug before running out the door. "Goodbye, Grandpa! Goodbye, Stanley!"

Annie clings to Grandpa and whispers as she looks up at him, "Grandpa, I'll always remember I'm God's little chick."

Grandpa kneels down to hug Annie. "That's very good, Annie. Your heavenly Father loves you, and you're always in His care. See you and Adam next Sunday!"

He whistles an old song called "Under His Wings" as he waves goodbye.

Parent/Teacher Guide

Descriptions of who God is:

- God calls every star and every child by name—Psalm 147:4; Isaiah 43:1

- God is Creator of heaven and earth; He's an Artist—Psalm 19:1

- God has no beginning and no end; no one made God—Psalm 93:2

- God is always with us—Psalm 139:7-10

- God is wise; no one teaches God—Job 12:13; Romans 11:33-36

- God thinks about us all day long—as many times as there are grains of sand —Psalm 139:17-18

- God is our heavenly Father, and He wants to have a personal relationship with us—Matthew 6:9; John 17:20-21

- We are in God's care, like a chick under its mother's wings—Psalm 91:4

- Jesus is God who came to earth; He is like a photograph of God —John 14:9; Hebrews 1:1-3

- God never changes; we can always count on Him—Hebrews 13:8

- Our Creator is also our Savior; He creates a new heart in us when we trust in Him—2 Corinthians 5:17; John 3:3

- The Bible is the only Book that comes straight from God. It teaches us who God is. Its truths are forever —Psalm 119:89, 98; Matthew 4:4